A PROBLEM
SHARED

TALKING ABOUT

SOCIAL MEDIA

Louise Spilsbury

W
FRANKLIN WATTS
LONDON•SYDNEY

Franklin Watts
First published in Great Britain in 2020 by The Watts Publishing Group
Copyright © The Watts Publishing Group, 2020

Series editor: Amy Pimperton
Design and illustration: Collaborate

HB ISBN: 978 1 4451 7130 2
PB ISBN: 978 1 4451 7131 9

FSC
www.fsc.org
MIX
Paper from
responsible sources
FSC® C104740

Printed and bound in China

Every attempt has been made to
clear copyright. Should there be
any inadvertent omission please
apply to the publisher for rectification.

Franklin Watts, an imprint of
Hachette Children's Group
Carmelite House
50 Victoria Embankment
London EC4Y 0DZ

An Hachette UK Company
www.hachette.co.uk
www.franklinwatts.co.uk

CONTENTS

SOCIAL MEDIA PROBLEMS

Many of us spend some time almost every day sharing, liking, tweeting and updating on one social media platform or another.

Using social media can be great – it puts the online world at our fingertips and allows us to stay in touch with friends, share photos and videos, and discover new things. Using social media is not always a good thing however, and it causes some people some very serious problems.

Problems with social media take different forms and everyone's experience of them will be different. These are a few examples of the ways it can affect people badly:

- stress
- anxiety
- bad moods or even depression
- lack of sleep
- low self-esteem
- loneliness.

SHARING PROBLEMS

Have you ever heard the saying 'A problem shared is a problem halved'? While there is no guarantee talking about a problem will reduce it by half, sharing our worries or concerns really does help us to feel better. It also gives other people the chance to help us.

If some aspect of social media is making someone feel low or lonely, or affecting their schoolwork or happiness, then the first step they should take is to tell someone about it. In this book we meet some people who have talked about problems with social media and find out what happened when they did.

FIND A BALANCE

Social media can be fun and useful, but it's important not to let it take over your life. Finding the right balance between it and schoolwork, exercise, sleeping well and having fun with friends and family is much better for your mind and body.

ZZZ

FOMO IS NO FUN

Many of us have passing feelings of missing out when we see a friend posting lots of cool stuff online, especially if we are having a bad day. But what if this fear of missing out starts to make you feel lonely and unwanted so badly that it makes you miserable. This is Finn's story.

Finn

I'm a quiet person and I have a couple of good mates who I like to play sport and hang out with, but I've always been happy with my own company, too. But recently, seeing everyone else's updates and photos online is making me feel left out. Everyone seems to have way more friends than me and they are always going out together or doing fun stuff.

I don't think people would want to be with me anyway as I must seem really boring in comparison. The worst thing was seeing pictures of my so-called best mate having a great time at a party. He hadn't even told me he was going. When he messaged me later to fetch me for a game of footie I blanked him. I'd rather stay in alone than be friends now.

If you feel left out and hide away at home feeling lonely and sad, that's a red flag, a sign that something is wrong and you need to talk to someone about it. Cutting yourself off from friends won't help your feelings of loneliness.

WHAT DO YOU THINK?

Do you think looking at social media sites too long or too often can affect your mood? Does seeing lots of pictures of other people having fun make you feel your life is a bit dull in comparison?

What do you think you should do if this happens?

TALK IT OUT

Finn's friend Rhys messages Finn a few more times. When Rhys doesn't get an answer, he goes round to Finn's house and refuses to leave until Finn talks to him. This is what happened next.

Rhys

When Finn didn't reply, I was worried something was wrong, so I went to see him. It's much easier to tell what someone is really thinking when you can see their face! I had no idea he'd seen the party pictures. I reminded him that he is always going on about hating parties. That's why I didn't mention it to him. I told him the party was way less fun than it looked in the pictures and I'd rather have been hanging out with him anyway!

In fact, the mate who had the party was feeling low himself because his parents are splitting up. The party was a fun way to forget all that for a bit. You can't believe everything you see on social media! Finn is a really good friend. I like that he is quiet and thoughtful and we have a laugh together, so I'm glad we sorted it out. We decided that if he feels like he wants to go to the next party then we can go together.

BE YOURSELF

We all like to socialise in different ways. Some people prefer to hang out in smaller groups or one-on-one. Other people love big parties and large groups of people. The important thing is to be yourself and to socialise in a way that makes you feel good.

TOP TIPS

When looking at posts and updates on social media ask yourself these questions:

- why do you think some people post only pictures of themselves having a great time?
- what has been cropped or edited out of the apparently 'perfect' pictures on show and why?
- do you think these people are really that happy all of the time?

TAKE TIME OUT

The urge to check social media platforms any time of the day and even all day can be tempting, but as Marcus discovered, it can also be unhealthy if it starts to take over your life.

Marcus

Mum is always joking that I'm addicted to social media and telling me to get off my phone. I do check it a lot, but that's because there are always a lot of updates coming in. Sometimes I think I'll just have a quick look and it takes longer than I realise, but I can't see a problem with it.

I guess I am on my phone for three hours a day, or at the weekend maybe five. I usually do it while the rest of the family talk, play games or watch TV. They get a bit grumpy about me not joining in much, but being online is a way to be in touch with my friends, which I like. It also gives me something to do at night because I find it really hard to get to sleep. I find it hard to stay asleep and I wake up a lot in the night, so I look at my phone then, too.

RED FLAG

Both the blue light of screens (which affects sleep quality), and the fact that people may wake to check their phones, reduces the number of hours of sleep many people get. If someone has bags under their eyes and is constantly yawning and feeling tired, these are red flags – signs that they are not getting the sleep they need to be healthy.

TALK ABOUT IT

Talk with your friends about how long you spend each day on social media. Do any of their parents set them a time limit? Can you think of three reasons why this might be a good idea? For example, you could spend more time on a hobby or exercising instead of sitting looking at a screen.

A DIGITAL DETOX!

Marcus's parents get a call from his school saying there is a problem. Marcus always seem to be tired and yawning at school, skips sports lessons, isn't concentrating in class and hasn't been handing in homework on time. His mum decides to take action.

Marcus's mum

I'd been worried Marcus was tired, but he never wants to talk these days. He just said things were fine when I asked. After the school called, we made a new family agreement: all devices to be switched off during mealtimes and for at least an hour before bed. No one is allowed to keep their phone by their bed overnight.

Although the rest of the family agreed, Marcus was really angry at first. He said he'd be missing out and would lose touch with his friends. But after a few weeks he realised that having a little less time on screen means he has more to talk about with them when he does go online. He seems happier, too. He has caught up on most of his schoolwork, has more energy because he sleeps better and spends time with us in the evening. I just wish we'd started the digital detox sooner!

TOP TIPS

DAILY REMINDER: 2 Hrs

Here are some great tips for digital detoxing:

- you can set daily reminders telling you how long you've been using an app, so you can make sure you save some time to spend with family and friends
- switch off notifications so that they aren't tempting you to check your device all the time
- phone-free time gives more time to try something new, such as painting, playing music or a new sport
- try listening to an audio book rather than reading on your phone
- on average you need nine to ten hours sleep a night to stay healthy. Stop screen use an hour before bed so your brain has time to wind down.

PICTURE PERFECT

When faced with a constant stream of photo-shopped images of so-called perfect people being liked online, anyone can feel insecure. Unfortunately, too much exposure to such images can make some people feel inadequate and it can seriously mess with their self-esteem. This is Neeta's story.

I started following some social media accounts to learn some make-up techniques. Then I sort of got hooked. Before I started following them, I didn't have a problem with the way I look, but now I find myself looking at more and more pictures of these slim, perfect and beautifully made-up people and wishing I looked like them and not like me.

Neeta

Even though I tell myself these pictures aren't real and the shots are all taken with filters and lighting and clever angles, I still feel fat, worthless and ugly. I feel uncomfortable going out because I feel so unconfident. I hate looking in the mirror and I even fantasise about getting cosmetic surgery to change the way I look. Some days I hate myself.

WHAT SHOULD NEETA DO?

1 Talk to a friend, family member or another trusted adult about how she is feeling?

2 Stop looking on social media altogether?

3 Make herself feel better about her body image by doing things like painting her nails and doing her hair?

THINK ABOUT IT

Think about the likely outcomes of the different options. Which suggestion is most likely to help Neeta in the long term? Does this help you decide which answer is best?

BODY POSITIVE

Neeta's friend Tara is sick of hearing Neeta complain about her body and her fixation with her weight and appearance. She waits until they are alone and tries to talk to Neeta about it.

Tara

Neeta used to be good fun, but recently she's been so negative about everything. She never wants to go out. She's always on her phone and just wants to take selfies. When I told her I wouldn't be able to hang out with her because of this, she got upset. She admitted that she knows the accounts she follows aren't making her happy, but she still keeps looking.

So, we had a hug and made a plan. We cleaned out her social media accounts of anyone she follows who doesn't make her feel good. We replaced them with body positivity sites that encourage people to love and respect what their amazing bodies do for them, no matter what shape or size they are. And we're going to focus on the many things we're good at instead of the way we look — and spend time having some real fun.

A SLIPPERY SLOPE

Many of the 'perfect' people you see on social media are influencers who are paid, or given things for free, to promote products and lifestyles. It's their job to get people to buy into their 'brand' and to spend real money on the products they promote. It can be a slippery slope where followers think that they have to spend more and more to be as 'perfect' as the influencers.

TOP TIPS

Constant comparisons can wear down your mental resilience. Here are some tips to help you to avoid the negative side of social media:

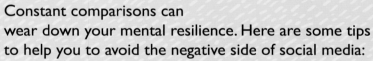

- spend time with people who make you feel good about yourself
- try not to compare yourself to images of people you see online, which are often digitally altered and don't reflect how they look in real life
- remember that many of the lifestyles shown on social media are actually adverts for you to buy stuff
- every time you think something negative about yourself, make yourself find something positive about yourself as well. If you think 'my hair's a mess today', counter that with 'nobody else cares about that and I love what I am wearing today!'.

PASSWORD PROBLEMS

Cyberbullying – when bullies insult or spread rumours about someone online or on social media – can be extremely distressing. Keeping your passwords and online identity private is one way to keep safe – as Mo found out.

Mo

I didn't think to keep my passwords a secret from Dan when we were mates. I guess I thought we'd be always be friends. After we fell out, Dan logged on to my accounts and set up a fake profile. He started impersonating me and posted really nasty messages and comments about other people as if they were from me.

Some people have stopped speaking to me or say horrible things about me or to my face. I think everyone hates me and no one believes me when I say the messages weren't from me. I'm so unhappy and feel so bad that some days I just pretend I'm ill so I can stay home from school. I spend a lot of time alone in my room and never let my mum and dad see my accounts in case they think it's me, too.

RED FLAG

When someone is sad and low, looks upset after using the Internet or their phone, spends a lot of time alone and is reluctant to let family members see their devices, this is a red flag. They might be being bullied online and need help.

TALK ABOUT IT

What do you think Mo should do? Talk about whether you think he should confront Dan and what you think might happen if he does. Do you think Dan's actions are a form of bullying? What is the advice usually given to victims of bullies?

A NEW PROFILE

Mo's older brother Zayn happens to see the account impersonating Mo and guesses what has happened. He persuades Mo that Dan is bullying him and that Mo should do something about it immediately.

Zayn

Mo was embarrassed he'd told Dan his password and was scared that Mum and Dad might confiscate his phone, but I persuaded him to tell them what was happening. Their main worry was what the bullying was doing to Mo.

They decided to go with Mo into school and tell the Head what is happening. They also phoned Dan's parents to tell them about it. At first, Dan's folks didn't believe us, but Dan broke down when they asked him and now he is grounded and had his phone taken away.

I helped Mo deactivate and delete all of his old accounts and start again with new passwords. We also reported Dan's bullying to apps and social networking sites. After the Head gave an assembly about cyberbullying and the dangers of being impersonated, most people believe Mo now. He seems fine, although he's definitely more careful online now!

Passwords are really important if you are using social media, so follow these tips for better safety:

- password protect your phone or tablet
- keep passwords safe and change them often
- don't let anyone watch you signing in and if they do, change the password as soon as you can
- never leave your computer without logging off or leave your phone lying around unlocked
- choose unusual passwords with a mix of letters, lowercase, uppercase, symbols and numbers. Don't use any part of your name, email address or your birth date.

THE 5 P'S

To keep your online accounts safe, learn about the 5 P's of online safety: **P**asswords, **P**rivacy settings, **P**ersonal information (don't give anyone details about yourself, your family, where you live or what school you go to), **P**rofiles and **P**adlocks.

21

MEETING PEOPLE ONLINE

Chatting to people online can be a great way to spend time and talk to friends, but talking to people you cannot see and don't know in real life has real dangers, as Celia found out.

Celia

I started going online a lot because I was feeling lonely. I'm quite shy and I find it hard to make friends with people at school. I like making new friends online because it's easier than talking to people face-to-face. It made me feel less lonely. I don't see a problem with adding people that I don't know because everyone I've met online so far seems really nice.

I got talking to Zac about three weeks ago and we hit it off from the start. We just seem to have so much in common, it's unbelievable. He's the same age as me and we like all the same music, games, and films and he is even shy like me. He sent photos of himself and he's really good-looking — he could be a model! I can't believe he likes me and I'm so lucky to have met him. He says he's not ready to meet yet, but I can wait — I'm sure he's worth it.

Look again at Celia's story. List all of the things that she says they have in common. Do you think this is a real coincidence? What do you think Celia should do next?

RED FLAG

When people are online they can hide who they really are. They might send you a photo or video they say is of themselves when it isn't actually them. What are the signs or red flags in Celia's story that might suggest she hasn't been careful enough and that Zac might not be a boy the same age as her?

ALARM BELLS RING

The only person Celia decides to tell about her online boyfriend is her best friend Holly, but Holly isn't happy about the relationship. Holly and Celia have a big bust-up when Celia accuses Holly of being jealous and then storms off.

Holly

At first it was good to see Celia so happy, but the more she told me about Zac, the more worried I got. It was all just too good to be true. I mean, nobody has exactly the same interests and problems as you and that photo looked like a screengrab!

Then she told me he was getting worried she didn't really like him and that he'd said the only the way she could prove she loved him was by sending him naked pictures of herself. Luckily she hasn't done that yet, but she's so scared of losing him I think she might.

He also said that maybe after she sends pictures of herself, they could meet up. When I said it all sounded dodgy and we should tell her parents, she lost her temper. She said I'm just jealous because no one like Zac loves me. I was angry and told her I didn't care what happened to her after that, but its not true. Now I don't know what to do.

WHAT SHOULD HOLLY DO?

1 Keep Celia's secret. Best friends do not tell each other's secrets, ever.

2 Stop seeing Celia – it sounds like she was really rude to Holly.

3 Talk to a trusted adult about Celia's situation and get help.

RED FLAG

Someone asking you to prove that you like or love them by sending a naked photo is a massive red flag. Once you send that photo you will have no control over who it could be sent to. The person you send it to could threaten to send it to your friends or family and use it to bribe you to do other things.

AGAINST THE LAW

Sending naked photographs of children is against the law. You could get into serious trouble if you send a naked photo of yourself or forward a photo of someone else.

25

THE AWFUL TRUTH

Holly bumps into Celia's dad, Peter, in the street and when he asks why they've fallen out, Holly blurts out the whole story. Celia's dad heads straight home.

When I got home and tried to talk to Celia about Zac, she got very embarrassed. She was furious with Holly for telling me. But then she seemed relieved to be talking about it. Deep down she had realised there was something off about the whole thing and that the stuff Zac asking her to do was making her feel very uneasy.

Peter

We got in touch with the police who took her computer and discovered that 'Zac' was actually a 40-year-old man who has done this kind of thing before and has even been in prison for it. Celia was incredibly upset, but we are all so relieved that he was stopped before something bad happened. Celia called Holly to thank her for looking out for her and now they are closer than ever. They are both more careful online than ever before.

Most people online are kind, normal people, but it is a good idea to take extra precautions, such as:

- only talk to real-life friends or family on social media sites and in chatrooms
- only join a private chatroom with people you already know. Online strangers are still strangers and could be pretending to be someone they are not!
- if anyone asks you to do something you feel uncomfortable about, delete or block that contact
- never arrange to meet people in real life that you've talked to only online, because you have no idea who they really are.

GROOMING

Grooming is when an adult contacts a child on the Internet with the aim of getting that child to meet them or send naked photos of themselves. Grooming is a crime in many countries.

BE SOCIAL MEDIA SAVVY

Using social media is a great way to stay in touch with friends, explore more about your hobbies and passions, and find and share all sorts of information and fun stuff. Make sure you can go on enjoying social media by doing what you need to stay safe online.

Make sure you use privacy settings wherever they exist to keep your information private and check them regularly.

Keep your apps up-to-date, too. Updates fix weaknesses in software, so installing them as soon as possible will help keep your devices safe from hackers or criminals.

Make sure that you don't publish personal information on social media, such as where you live, where you are, your email address, phone number or date of birth, in case someone tries to trace you.

When you're online, check how you're feeling now and then. Before you post or comment ask yourself: 'Am I doing something positive for myself and the people who'll see it?'.

If someone upsets or bullies you, don't be tempted to reply. This could make matters worse. If the bullying continues, keep copies of the messages and posts and report the bully to the service provider to get it stopped.

If something upsets you online, switch off and talk to someone in real life. Limiting online time and taking more time in the real world can help you feel better.

TOP TIPS

Be very careful about what images and messages you post, even among trusted friends – once they are online they can be shared widely and are extremely difficult to get removed. It's a good idea never to post anything you would be worried about a teacher or a grandparent seeing!

GLOSSARY

addicted to be dependent on something

anxiety feeling worried, nervous or scared about something

confiscate to (officially) take something away from someone

depression a mental health condition where a person feels low or sad for all or some of the time

detox to avoid or stop doing something that is harmful; a digital detox is when you avoid using devices for a period of time

exposure to come into contact with something, which is often harmful

fixation a strong interest or obsession with something

impersonate to pretend to be someone else

inadequate lacking

insecure uncertain and anxious; unconfident

resilience the ability to recover quickly from difficulties

self-esteem how you feel about yourself; your confidence

service provider a company that gives you access to the Internet

stress mental or emotional strain or tension

updates they ensure devices are working on the newest versions of sofware

urge a strong desire or impulse

FURTHER INFORMATION

BOOKS

Get Ahead in Computing: Super Social Media and Awesome Online Safety by Clive Gifford (Wayland, 2019)

Teen Life Confidential: Texts, Tweets, Trolls and Teens by Anita Naik (Wayland, 2014)

Your Mind Matters: Social Media and You by Honor Head (Franklin Watts, 2020)

WEBSITES

ChildLine has an excellent section on online and mobile phone safety and spotting the signs of online grooming. The website is packed with useful and practical tips and advice.
www.childline.org.uk/info-advice/bullying-abuse-safety/online-mobile-safety/

Internet Matters is a site dedicated to all things online. Advice can filtered by age and it covers everything from screen time to online grooming across a range of devices. It also has lots of resources for teachers and parents.
www.internetmatters.org/

The Young Minds website offers advice and support to help with social media problems and has advice on how social media can impact on your mental health.
www.youngminds.org.uk/find-help/looking-after-yourself/social-media-and-mental-health/

HELPLINES

Text the YoungMinds Crisis Messenger for free 24/7 support across the UK. If you need urgent help text **YM** to **85258**. All texts are answered by trained volunteers, with support from experienced clinical supervisors.

ChildLine is a counselling service for children and young people. You can contact ChildLine in these ways: by phone on **0800 1111**, send an email, have a 1-2-1 chat with them, send a message to Ask Sam and you can post messages to the ChildLine message boards. You can contact ChildLine about anything – no problem is too big or too small. Find out more at **www.childline.org.uk/get-support/**

Kids Helpline is Australia's free, private and confidential helpline for kids. If you are experienceing social media issues, such as cyberbullying, you can contact them on **1800 55 1800**.

INDEX